The Ultimate Financial
Breakthrough

The Ultimate Financial Breakthrough

Pastor E A Adeboye

Published by Roper Penberthy Publishing Ltd
Springfield House, 23 Oatlands Drive, Weybridge, Surrey KT13 9LZ

All Bible quotations are from the Authorised (King James) Version of the Holy Bible.

This Edition published 2010
First published 2005

ISBN 978 1 903905 65 4

Initially published by Christ the Redeemer's Ministries
Contact Address:
Redeemed Christian Church of God, Central Office UK, Redemption House, Station Road, Knebworth, Hertfordshire SG3 6AT
United Kingdom

Cover design by Audri Coleman

Typeset by Avocet Typeset, Chilton, Aylesbury, Buckinghamshire

Printed in India by Imprint Digital

Compliments On Pastor E.A. Adeboye's 70th Birthday Celebration

God Bless You!

2.3.2012

+ Olu Adeboye

Table of Contents

1 Ultimate Financial Breakthrough   9

2 Givers Never Lack   23

3 Secrets of Abundance   29

4 From Abject Poverty to Wealth   39

5 Steps To Unlimited Greatness   51

6 The Key to Abundance   59

7 Sacrificial Giving   65

8 The Pathway To Riches   75

9 The Turnaround Miracle   83

10 Uncommon Prosperity   89

Foreword

God specializes in using the little things of this world to lead people into greatness. This is one way He shows that He is the Almighty.

He wants to lead you into a place of abundant wealth.
This is the season of the ultimate breakthrough. God will lift you up above your expectations. He will bless you with unprecedented financial blessings.

E. A. Adeboye
December 2005.

Chapter One

———◆———

ULTIMATE FINANCIAL BREAKTHROUGH

And the word of the LORD came unto him, saying,

"Arise, get thee to Zarephath, which belongeth to Zidon, and dwell there: behold, I have commanded a widow woman there to sustain thee."

So he arose and went to Zarephath.

And when he came to the gate of the city, behold, the widow woman was there gathering of sticks: and he called to her, and said, Fetch me, I pray thee, a little water in a vessel, that I may drink.

And as she was going to fetch it, he called to her, and said, Bring me, I pray thee, a morsel of bread in thine hand.

And she said, As the LORD thy God liveth, I have not a cake, but an handful of meal in a barrel, and a little oil in a cruse: and, behold, I am gathering two sticks, that I may go in and dress it for me and my son, that we may eat it, and die.

And Elijah said unto her, Fear not: go and do as thou hast said: but make me thereof a little cake first, and bring it unto me, and after make for thee and for thy son.

For thus saith the LORD God of Israel, The barrel of meal shall not waste, neither shall the cruse of oil fail, until the day that the LORD sendeth rain upon the earth.

And she went and did according to the saying of Elijah: and she, and he, and her house, did eat many days.

And the barrel of meal wasted not, neither did the cruse of oil fail, according to the word of the LORD, which he spake by Elijah. 1 Kings 17:8-16

The ways of God are very simple. Biblical principles enable us to achieve unusual breakthroughs with ease. There are breakthroughs and there are ultimate breakthroughs. When we talk about the ultimate breakthrough, we refer to the breakthrough which swallows up all other breakthroughs.

God can give you, the ultimate financial breakthrough. He can transform your finances to a realm where the thoughts of poverty will be completely banished from your mind. It is God's intention to pour on His sons and daughters the ultimate financial breakthrough.

THE SECRETS

God has raised up several multi-millionaires as a result of the monthly Divine Encounter programme. That is why I wrote this book. Its main thrust is to lay bare before you the secrets of ultimate financial breakthrough. Its pages contain unusual wisdom, which will lead you to the peak of financial breakthrough. God is not interested in leading you to modest breakthroughs. He wants to take you to the peak. The secrets of explosive financial breakthroughs can be summed up in this sentence:- "Knowing what to do in order to get the best result and then doing it". The story of the widow of Zarephath illustrates this principle beautifully. The widow was told what to do and she carried out the instructions given to her.

You may ask, "What must I do to prosper continuously and attain the level of ultimate financial breakthrough?"
The story of the widow of Zarephath answers the question. You can move from a zero to a hero very quickly. You may start from the most humble beginnings and still reach the peak of financial abundance. In other words, the poorest can become the richest. The man who currently lives a hand-to-mouth existence can become a benefactor to hundreds and thousands of people.

I have yet to come across someone that is as poor as the widow in question. She was so poor that she had only one meal left to eat before dying of hunger. From this starting point, the Almighty raised her up to a point where she never lacked anything again. Based on the teaching of this passage, I say to anyone who reads this book that you can be so enriched by God that you will be able to feed a whole city.

THE PRINCIPLES

Seven principles derive from the story of the widow of Zarephath. These principles, tried and tested, are God's blueprint for securing the ultimate financial breakthrough. If you follow the principles, you will move from your present level of wealth to the peak of financial freedom and sufficiency. God will so shower you with abundant financial resources that besides enjoying a comfortable lifestyle, you will have the resources to finance projects in the church and in your community. You will move from the level of those who manage meagre resources to those who eat what they want, buy what they want, live comfortably and have more than sufficient to provide for the needs of others. In this world of economic recession and scarce resources, it is possible to become a recipient of great blessing. The Almighty can easily locate you and make you a recipient of the ultimate financial breakthrough. All you need is to follow these seven principles:

1. Sow When It Is Practically Difficult To Do So:

The widow of Zarephath sowed when it was exceptionally inconvenient for her – she sowed the last thing she had. It is quite easy to give out of your abundance and easier still to give away things which you no longer need. But the giver who is going to be particularly blessed by God is the one who gives when it hurts.

The level of giving is not measured by what is given, but by what is left after one has given. Many people were casting their offerings when Jesus visited the temple but the Lord singled out a particular widow. The widow did not give much, but because she gave all that she had, Jesus declared her to be the greatest giver of them all.

And Jesus sat over against the treasury, and beheld how the people cast money into the treasury: and many that were rich cast in much.

And there came a certain poor widow, and she threw in two mites, which make a farthing.

And he called unto him his disciples, and saith unto them, Verily I say unto you, That this poor widow hath cast more in, than all they which have cast into the treasury:

For all they did cast in of their abundance; but she of her want did cast in all that she had, even all her living. Mark 12:41-44

This widow had no husband to provide for her. He died leaving nothing behind hence, she became poor. A mite is the smallest Jewish coin valued at about one- fourth of an American cent. What she gave seemed insignificant.

This kind of giving also characterised the Corinthian believers, who gave in spite of their deep poverty:

How that in a great trial of affliction the abundance of their joy and their deep poverty abounded unto the riches of their liberality.

For to their power, I bear record, yea, and beyond their power they were willing of themselves; 2 Corinthians 8:2-3

Even if you are poor today, God can make you richer than the richest man in your community. If you put into practice the type of giving exemplified by the widow, you can give your way to prosperity by offering the type of gifts which God delights in. If widows can give all that they have, why do people who are in a better financial state not give more? God is looking for sacrificial givers:- those who will give even when it is not convenient.

Every man according as he purposeth in his heart so let him give, not grudgingly, or of necessity: for God loveth a cheerful giver. 2 Corinthians 9:7

If you want to attract God's attention with giving, give when it is not convenient and God will bless you in an extraordinary manner. Solomon laid bare the secret of his success and wealth in the passage below;

He that observeth the wind shall not sow; and he that regardeth the clouds shall not reap.

As thou knowest not what is the way of the spirit, nor how the bones do grow in the womb of her that is with child: even so thou knowest not the works of God who maketh all.

In the morning sow thy seed, and in the evening withhold not thine hand: for thou knowest not whether shall prosper, either this or that, or whether they both shall be alike good. Ecclesiastes 11:4-6

Here we discover the secret of Solomon's abundant wealth. He was an incurable giver. You can be one too if you do not wait until it is convenient to give. Sow even when you face financial challenges. Sow in the morning, in the afternoon and in the evening. Keep on sowing and God will keep on blessing you.

2. **Sow On Good Ground:** The widow of Zarephath sowed

on a very fertile ground.

Sowing on good ground is illustrated by the parable of the sower and the seed.

Hearken; Behold, there went out a sower to sow:

And it came to pass, as he sowed, some fell by the way side, and the fowls of the air came and devoured it up.

And some fell on stony ground, where it had not much earth, and immediately it sprang up, because it had no depth of earth:

"But when the sun was up, It was scorched; and because it had no root, it withered away.

And some fell among thorns, and the thorns grew up, and choked it, and it yielded no fruit.

And other fell on good ground, and did yield fruit that sprang up and increased; and brought forth, some thirty, and some sixty, and some an hundred. Mark 4:3-8

Here, the Bible tells us that there are various grounds to sow on. The type of ground on which you sow will determine your yield or output. The widow of Zarephath sowed on the best ground. She had only one seed to sow yet she knew that it mattered where she sowed the seed for it would be critical in determining her harvest. She identified a very fertile ground and sowed on it.

The unwise sow by the roadside, among the thorns and on stony ground. The wise, on the other hand, ensure that they sow on good soil. Those who sow on good ground come up with three levels of bountiful harvest

- The thirty-fold return
- The sixty-fold return
- The hundredfold return

The type of giving which achieves results can be classified into the three categories above. The thirty- fold return is secured by those who give to members of the household of faith.

And let us not be weary in well doing: for in due season we shall reap, if we faint not

As we have therefore opportunity, let us do good unto

all men, especially unto them who are of the household of faith. Galations 6:9-10

Each gift you offer to the brethren will attract the thirty- fold return. The sixty-fold return is achieved when you give to pastors, prophets, evangelists and other men and women of God.

He that receiveth a prophet in the name of a prophet shall receive a prophet's reward; and he that receiveth a righteous man in the name of a righteous man shall receive a righteous man's reward Matthew 10:41

To achieve the hundredfold return, you must give to the high priest. In other words, you are not only expected to give to the prophet but to the head of the sons of the prophets.

The widow of Zarephath sowed into the life of Elijah. Thus, she was able to access the source of superabundant blessings as she reaped a hundredfold return. She was not only supplied with food to eat for the rest of her life, but also had death expelled when it was trying to kill her only child. When you sow into the life of a high priest, you do not only get monetary returns, you also are blessed with things which money cannot buy.

A WISE GIVER

Let me share some, striking testimonies with you. A young man once walked into my office and said: "I want to give you a house". I gave him a terse reply "I don't need your house. I already have my own house". Because I live in the redemption camp, I explained to him that I did not need a house in the city where the house he wished to give me was located. The man insisted that I must receive the gift but I insisted I would not.

In his desire to convince me, he told me that he had two houses and that giving one to me one was fine by him. I told him that I know some pastors who would gladly accept such a gift and that I could give him their names. He absolutely insisted that he must give this house to me. When I saw his determination, I told him to go home and pray and to come back after three months.

Three months later, he came and said, "I have prayed and I'm convinced that God wants me to give you the house. The keys are here". I prayed and asked God to tell me what to do. God told me to accept the gift and I did. In the course of making enquiries, I discovered that one of the branches of the Redeemed Christian Church Of God needed accommodation in the immediate vicinity of that house and I willingly offered it to them to make use of it for Church services.

Within a short time, the man came back with a request. He asked "Will you kindly come with me?" I obliged. He took me to a place where there was a very big estate. Beaming with smiles, the young man said "This is what the Lord has done for me. I want you to dedicate this estate to His glory". Displaying a fatherly sense of humour I said, "Young man, you must be very smart. You gave God a house and you got an estate". If the young man had held on to his house, he wouldn't have ever remotely become the owner of an estate.

DIVINE INTERVENTION

A particular sister took on the responsibility of attending to my needs during my visits to a town in Western Nigeria. During one of those visits, I met the sister at the place where she parked her car but she was in a very despondent frame of mind. I questioned in my mind why she was standing beside her car so downcast. Initially, I thought that her car had developed a problem but when I asked to know what the matter was, she replied, "There is no problem with the car, but something is wrong with me". What was wrong with her was that she had suffered a miscarriage. An eight-month old baby had died in her womb and doctors were planning to flush out the dead baby. She stood there sorrowful and depressed. I laid hands on her womb and called on the Almighty to intervene. Within a few minutes, the baby came back to life and God restored to this sister what the enemy had tried to steal from her. The same God who gave life to a dead baby in the womb will visit you with His resurrection power today in the name of Jesus.

Chapter Two

GIVERS NEVER LACK

If you are an avid reader of the Bible you would have discovered that God specializes in performing special miracles when those who give sacrificially call upon Him for intervention. The story of the Shunammite woman teaches us vital lessons, one of which is that givers will always secure heaven's attention. When you meet God's needs He will also meet your needs supernaturally and promptly.

And it fell on a day, that Elisha passed to Shunem, where was a great woman; and she constrained him to eat bread. And so it was, that as oft as he passed by, he turned in thither to eat bread.

And she said unto her husband, Behold now, I perceive that this is an holy man of God, which passeth by us continually.

Let us make a little chamber, I pray thee, on the wall; and let us set for him there a bed, and a table, and a stool, and a candlestick: and it shall be, when he cometh to us, that he shall turn in thither.

And it fell on a day, that he came thither, and he turned into the chamber, and lay there.

And he said to Gehazi his servant, Call this Shunammite. And when he had called her, she stood before him.

And he said unto him, Say now unto her, Behold, thou has been careful for us with all this care; what is to be done for thee? wouldest thou be spoken for to the king, or to the captain of the host? And she answered, I dwell among mine own people.

And he said, What then is to be done for her? And Gehazi answered,

Verily she hath no child, and her husband is old.

And he said, Call her. And when he had called her, she stood in the door.

And he said, About this season, according to the time of life, thou shalt embrace a son. And she said, Nay, my lord, thou man of God, do not lie unto thine handmaid.
And the woman conceived, and bare a son at that season that Elisha had said unto her, according to the time of life. 2 Kings 4:8-17

The Shunammite woman took care of Elisha on many occasions when he passed by. She demonstrated uncommon commitment to ensuring that he was well catered for at all times. She never missed an opportunity to take care of the man of God. And so one day, the spirit of God told Elisha to ask the Shunammite woman what she needed. She stated that she needed a child and the man of God prophesied that a gift that money could not buy would be given to her.

He told her that she would have a baby within nine months. God's word given through Elijah was fulfilled, and the Shunammite woman became a mother nine months later.

And he said, About this season, according to the time of life, thou shalt embrace a son. And she said, Nay, my lord, thou man of God, do not lie unto thine handmaid.

And the woman conceived, and bare a son at that season that Elisha had said unto her, according to the time of life. 2 Kings 4:16-17

Givers always experience unprecedented miracles. When you give sacrificially, God will make the impossible to become possible in your life. This reminds me of a brother I met during one of my ministerial trips to the Eastern Nigeria. The brother picked me up at the airport having taken on the responsibility of driving me everywhere I went during the course of my visit. When it was time to leave, I tried to think of a parting gift I could give in appreciation of his hospitality. I knew it was difficult to give him cash gifts because he was so rich – so rich that I even jokingly thought he could buy me if I was offered for sale.

THE MIRACLE GIFT

But all the same, I gave him some money and said, "Brother, kindly give this small gift to your children". His response shocked me. He shouted "Amen" continuously and prayerfully. I called the pastor-in- charge of that province to find out why the brother was so enthusiastic about the gift I offered his children. The pastor informed me that although the brother was so rich, he was childless. I told the pastor that God was going to surprise him with a miracle.

When I visited the same city the following year, the rich brother was at the airport as usual to pick me up. On that particular occasion, he came with a surprise gift. With tears of joy streaming down his face, he declared, "This is a gift from my first son". The rich brother who had been childless for a number of years had become a proud father miraculously. By offering to drive me in his car, and believing the word of the Lord, the reproach of childlessness was rolled away from his life.

You can start giving sacrificially this very day and I assure you; the Lord will bless you beyond your wildest dreams. Wait patiently for His time because as far as giving is concerned, there is always a waiting time.

WAITING TIME

There is a time span between seedtime and harvest. The time between sowing and harvesting could be short or long depending on the type of seed that is sown. If the seed is significant, you may have to wait for some time before you reap the harvest. The Bible says:

Be patient therefore, brethren, unto the coming of the Lord. Behold, the husbandman waiteth for the precious fruit of the earth, and hath long patience for it, until he receive the early and latter rain. James 5:7

Farmers are never in a hurry. They know that they must wait for the harvest if they are to enjoy a good yield. Some believers are of the opinion that one can sow in the morning and reap in the evening. It is quite possible, but it depends on what you want to harvest. Some crops can be harvested within three to six months, while others may require more than one year before the farmer can harvest them.

There is no magic in farming as there are set procedures for planting and harvesting. A farmer plants a seed; it dies and sprouts again. Then within a certain period, it grows until it bears fruit. It is at this stage that the farmers begin to harvest. And likewise, you must wait for the time of harvest. If you sow on a good ground, as the Lord lives, the harvest will surely come in the name of Jesus.

Chapter Three

———◆———

SECRETS OF ABUNDANCE

I learnt some valuable lessons some years ago. When the crowd of participants at the monthly Holy Ghost service began to increase, I took a decision. Because I could no longer handle the crowd single-handedly, I selected seven elders and gave each one of them neckties that I had used during previous ministrations. "Put on these neckties; they are already soaked with God's anointing from the previous times of ministration," I told them. Whenever they wore those neckties and ministered, supernatural miracles always took place.

Signs and wonders happened through their ministry but something else happened as a result. I was showered with gifts of neckties. Every time people who were close to me were travelling, they came back with just one gift: neckties. If they travel to South Africa, the only gifts they bought for me were neckties. And when they travelled to America or London, again, they would bring neckties for me. Then I asked God, "Why are these people just giving me neckties? Can't they come up with other gifts beside neckties?"

PRECIOUS HARVEST

God gave me an insight into what was happening. He said, "Son, if you sow ties, you will reap ties". I quickly learnt the message and decided to start sowing shoes. I located pastors who wore the same size of shoes as me, and I gave a good number of shoes to them, among which were some of my best shoes. I expected a harvest of new ones immediately during the first month, but there were no gifts of shoes for me. When another month rolled by and there were still no gift of shoes for me, I went to God and said "You told me that if I sow, I would reap". It was then that the Lord taught me another lesson. He said, "Son if you plant maize, you can harvest it within three months, but if you plant yams, you will wait a little longer.

"Shoes are of greater value than ties; so the greater the quality of the seed sown, the more time you have to spend waiting for the harvest. You have planted shoes and you will have to wait a little longer, but the moment the harvest starts, there will be no stopping it". And then it came; I was showered with shoes of all sizes and colours: big shoes, small shoes, white shoes, green shoes, black shoes and all kinds of sophisticated shoes. When the harvest came in full, I was pleasantly surprised. If you have sowed any seed, your harvest will soon come. Just wait a little and your harvest will locate you in the name of Jesus.

You Must Work Hard: If you want to experience the ultimate financial breakthrough, you must be prepared for hard work. God may grant you the open window of financial favour, but it will be your responsibility to work towards reaching the pinnacle of financial abundance.
And to do this, you will be required to do a great deal of hard work.

The Bible says:

But without faith it is impossible to please him: for he that cometh to God must believe that he is, and that he is a rewarder of them that diligently seek him. Hebrews 11:6

Diligence in hard work is always rewarded, farmers must work hard if they are to reap a bountiful harvest. When farmers sow seeds, they begin to grow. But as they grow, weeds also grow side by side with them. Besides nurturing the good seed, you must also work hard to get rid of the weeds. You are not only expected to work hard, but also to pray hard.

Anyone who desires an encounter with the Almighty, which would culminate into the ultimate financial breakthrough, must be ready to work hard and pray hard. The Bible says;

I have planted, Apollos watered; but God gave the increase.

So then neither is he that planteth any thing, neither he that watereth; but God that giveth the increase. 1 Corinthians 3:6-7

Paul may plant and Apollos may water but it is God alone who gives the increase. You must learn to pray hard and call upon God to give you increase. Lazy people cannot experience the ultimate financial breakthrough.

Those who are not prepared to work and pray hard are not

yet ready for any form of meaningful financial breakthrough.

Put God First: When your harvest begins, you must remember to put God first. The Bible says;

Honour the Lord with thy substance, and with the firstfruits of all thine increase: So shall thy barns be filled with plenty, and thy presses shall burst out with new wine. Proverbs 3: 9-10

The Bible commands that we must honour God with our firstfruits. Some people gather in a harvest and allow the proceeds to waste away. Until you learn to honour God with your goods, you will not be able to benefit even from the harvest you have laboured to gather in. The Bible warns:

Is it time for you, O ye, to dwell in your ceiled houses, and this house lie waste?

Now therefore thus saith the LORD of hosts; Consider your ways.

Ye have sown much, and bring in little, ye eat, but ye have not enough; ye drink, but ye are not filled with drink; ye clothe you, but there is none warm, and he that earneth wages earneth wages to put it into a bag with holes.

Thus saith the LORD of hosts; Consider your ways.

Go up to the mountain, and bring wood, and build the house; and I will take pleasure in it, and I will be glorified, saith the LORD.

Ye looked for much, and, lo, it came to little; and when ye brought it home, I did blow upon it. Why? saith the LORD of hosts. Because of mine house that is waste, and ye run every man unto his own house.

Therefore the heaven over you is stayed from dew, and the earth is stayed from her fruit. And I called for a drought upon the land, and upon the mountains, and upon the corn, and upon the new wine, and upon the oil, and upon that which the ground bringeth forth, and upon men, and upon cattle, and upon all the labour of the hands. Haggai 1:4-11

Some people gather their harvests and put them in bags with holes. The problem of leaking bags results from a failure to honour God through giving Him the first fruits of our harvest. If you do not give to God, you may end up frittering away the proceeds of your harvest. Those who harvest into bags with holes are those who refuse to put God first.

Keep Sowing: If you want to experience the ultimate financial breakthrough, you must keep sowing. The first seed you sow may open the door to blessings, but it takes persistent sowing to keep the door of blessings open.

Let us take a look at the story of the widow of Zarephath once again. What opened the door of blessings to her was the first cake she made for Elijah, but what kept the food flowing was the fact that everyday, she kept on making cakes for Elijah. Your initial act of giving can take you to a certain level of financial breakthrough. But what will lead you to the level of ultimate financial breakthrough is persistent giving.

If by the third day, the widow of Zarephath had stopped giving, then her own source of supply would have dried up. Let us also learn a lesson from Solomon's example. The first time he sacrificed unto God, he offered a thousand offerings.

God prospered Him in no small measure as a mighty harvest

was unleashed upon him. The next time he sacrificed unto God, he offered twenty two thousand oxen.

And Solomon offered a sacrifice of peace offerings, which he offered unto the LORD, two and twenty thousand oxen, and an hundred and twenty thousand sheep. So the king and all the children of Israel dedicated the house of the LORD. 1 Kings 8:63

Solomon kept on increasing in wealth because he kept on giving. And at the end, he attained the level of ultimate financial breakthrough. He became so rich that nobody could attempt to count the amount of silver which he had.

EXPLOSIVE WEALTH

Someone who reads this book will become so rich that higher denominations like the one hundred dollar note, the one thousand Naira note and the five hundred Naira note will be the only ones that matter. When your workers bring you the proceeds from your business, you will tell them to hand you the higher denominations and keep the lower denominations for their own benefit.

What is the mystery behind the giving done by the widow of

Zarephath? It is uncommon faith in God. It is this faith that made her to give her only means of sustenance. She gave her only food to Elijah because she needed to surrender her future into the hands of the God of Elijah.

To make these secrets of the ultimate financial breakthrough work for you, you must first give your life to Jesus. You must surrender your life to Him today if you have not done so already. Today can become your moment of breakthrough. This is the hour of decision.

PRAYER GUIDE

1. Father, I hand over my life to you; take care of my future in the name of Jesus.

2. Hold up a special offering as you say this prayer: Father with this offering, open the door to my prosperity in the name of Jesus.

3. Father, I need the grace to keep on sowing so that the door of my prosperity will remain open, give it to me in Jesus name.

Chapter Four

---◆---

FROM ABJECT POVERTY TO WEALTH

The Bible has given us simple guidelines to follow regarding what it takes to achieve the ultimate financial breakthrough. Performing signs, wonders and miracles is one of God's great pleasures. Wherever there is a need, God presents himself at the scene to meet it. Your needs provide God with opportunities to demonstrate His greatness. Any embarrassing situation is an opportunity for God to demonstrate His supreme power and ability and to turn seemingly hopeless situations around. God does not need to exert Himself in order to make you rich. He can turn a pauper into a millionaire overnight and He is able to take you from abject poverty to the greatest imaginable level of wealth.

If you study the Bible regularly, you would have discovered through divine inspiration, that the presence of God in any situation follows a predictable pattern. When God comes into circumstances, a creditor will become a lender to nations; a widow will become the richest person in the community; those who live on proceeds from the rich will begin to lend to the rich. A man who is living under the bondage of debt can, with God's help, end up with resources to lend to institutes or banks. All these can happen, but only after a decisive encounter with the Almighty.

HOPE FOR THE HOPELESS

There is a beautiful story in the scriptures which illustrates the fact that the poorest can become the richest and that an outcast can become a celebrity. When you have an encounter with God and you carry out the divine instructions given to you during that encounter, your story would become a reference which people will later use to demonstrate the wonders of God.

A widow who had lost every hope had an encounter with

God when she came across Elisha the prophet. She was blessed with a miracle which altered the course of her life.

Now there cried a certain woman of the wives of the sons of the prophets unto Elisha, saying, Thy servant my husband is dead; and thou knowest that thy servant did fear the LORD: and the creditor is come to take unto him my two sons to be bondmen.

And Elisha said unto her, What shall I do for thee? tell me, what hast thou in the house? And she said, Thine handmaid hath not any thing in the house, save a pot of oil.

Then he said, Go, borrow thee vessels abroad of all thy neighbours, even empty vessels; borrow not a few.

And when thou art come in, thou shalt shut the door upon thee and upon thy sons, and shalt pour out into all those vessels, and thou shalt set aside that which is full.

So she went from him, and shut the door upon her and upon her sons, who brought the vessels to her; and she poured out.
And it came to pass, when the vessels were full, that she

said unto her son, Bring me yet a vessel. And he said unto her, There is not a vessel more. And the oil stayed.

Then she came and told the man of God. And he said, Go, sell the oil, and pay thy debt, and live thou and thy children of the rest. 2 Kings 4:1-7

There are certain lessons to be learnt from the account of this widow. Let us observe them.

1. **She cried out desperately for help:** The widow cried out to Elisha. From this, we learn that the journey to the realm of ultimate financial breakthrough starts with a desperate cry to God. God is eager to intervene in the affairs of those who cry unto him for help.

   And ye shall seek me, and find me, when ye shall search for me with all your heart. Jeremiah 29:13

Those who seek God with all their heart will find him. As long as you are content to remain in your present condition, your cry to God will be far from being desperate.

But when you really despair of your situation, you will cry out to God desperately. The Bible did not tell us that the widow had a chat with Elisha but that she cried unto Him because she was in desperate need of a miracle. Again we are not told that the widow murmured before Elisha, but that she cried. Nor are we told that she grumbled to attract the attention of the prophet of God; rather, she cried out for divine intervention.

2. **God answered through his servant:** Each time you cry to God, He will grant your request. The woman cried out and the man of God asked "What can I do for you?" God will answer your cry because the Bible says;

   Offer unto God thanksgiving; and pay thy vows unto the most High:

   And call upon me in the day of trouble: I will deliver thee, and thou shalt glorify me. Ps 50:14-15

God has declared in His word that if you cry to Him, He will answer you. He did not say that if you cry to Him, He will ignore you. God will not pretend that He does not hear you when you cry to Him; He will hear and will answer. The man of God, Elisha, asked the woman what she wanted. She made her request very simple and God met her at the point of that request.

God will answer you today in the name of Jesus.

3. **God directed her:** The man of God gave her certain specific instructions: She was told to borrow empty vessels from her neighbours and was given a step by step guideline on how to obtain her breakthrough. Your journey into prominence will begin today and God will guide you step by step in Jesus name.

Whenever God wants to give someone a major breakthrough, He guides that person. Hence, you must pay attention when God speaks, and listen carefully for His instructions. Read what the Bible says here:-

And it came to pass, that, as the people pressed upon him to hear the word of God, he stood by the lake of Gennesaret,

And saw two ships standing by the lake: but the fishermen were gone out of them, and were washing their nets.

And he entered into one of the ships, which was Simon's, and prayed him that he would thrust out a little from the land. And he sat down, and taught the people out of the ship.

Now when he had left speaking, he said unto Simon, Launch out into the deep, and let down your nets for a draught.

And Simon answering said unto him, Master, we have toiled all the night and have taken nothing: nevertheless at thy word I will let down the net.

And when they had this done, they inclosed a great multitude of fishes: and their net brake.

And they beckoned unto their partners, which were in the other ship, that they should come and help them. And they came, and filled both the ships, so that they began to sink. Luke 5:1-7

Here Jesus told Peter to launch into the deep, and to throw his nets in a particular direction. If Peter had failed to obey this divine instruction, he would have missed the miracle. If you are willing to obey God, He will guide you one step at a time until you reach your breakthrough.

4. **God blessed her in her neighbourhood:** The woman was living in a predominantly poor neighbourhood. Looking at the story more closely, we can deduce that

most of her neighbours were very poor, for they had many empty vessels to spare. It was in the midst of these same neighbours that she found her greatest opportunity. Note this: you are living in the midst of opportunities. Where you live right now is where your miracles can happen. God will inspire you, and like that widow, you will find miracles happening in your neighbourhood.

In Genesis 26: 1-14, we come across an interesting story.

And there was a famine in the land, beside the first famine that was in the days of Abraham. And Isaac went unto Abimelech king of the Philistines unto Gerar.

And the LORD appeared unto him, and said, Go not down into Egypt; dwell in the land which I shall tell thee of:

Sojourn in this land, and I will be with thee, and will bless thee; for unto thee, and unto thy seed, I will give all these countries, and I will perform the oath which I sware unto Abraham thy father;

And I will make thy seed to multiply as the stars of heaven, and will give unto thy seed all these countries; and in thy seed shall all the nations of the earth be blessed;

Because that Abraham obeyed my voice, and kept my charge, my commandments, my statutes, and my laws. And Isaac dwelt in Gerar:

And the men of the place asked him of his wife; and he said, She is my sister: for he feared to say, She is my wife; lest, said he, the men of the place should kill me for Rebekah; because she was fair to look upon.

And it came to pass, when he had been there a long time, that Abimelech king of the Philistines looked out at a window, and saw, and, behold, Isaac was sporting with Rebekah his wife.

And Abimelech called Isaac, and said, Behold, of a surety she is thy wife: and how saidst thou, She is my sister? And Isaac said unto him, Because I said, Lest I die for her.

And Abimelech said, What is this thou hast done unto us? one of the people might lightly have lien with thy wife, and thou shouldest have brought guiltiness upon us. And Abimelech charged all his people, saying, He that toucheth this man or his wife shall surely be put to death.

Then Isaac sowed in that land, and received in the same

year an hundredfold: and the LORD blessed him. And the man waxed great, and went forward, and grew until he became very great:

For he had possession of flocks, and possessions of herds, and great store of servants: and the Philistines envied him.
Genesis 26:1-14

There was a famine in the land and Isaac was keen to move out of his neighbourhood. But God specifically told him to stay where he was and to sow there. He did this, and God prospered him in that land ravaged by famine. In the same vein, God is going to prosper you no matter how deep the economic recession in your neighbourhood or in your country. There is a river in your neighbourhood that harbours a particular fish; this fish has a gold coin in its belly. All you have to do is to catch the fish, open its mouth and claim the gold coin that will enrich you for life.

There are some people in your neighbourhood who have more money than they can ever spend in a lifetime. You only need to reach out to them with the message of salvation. Those who happen to be extremely rich are hungry for the message of salvation.

BOMBARDED WITH BLESSINGS

I am reminded of the story of a young lady who walked up to me and asked, "What would you like me to give you for Christmas?" I replied that she was free to give me whatever she can afford. When she repeatedly asked me what I wanted, I gave her an answer which I thought would stop the conversation. I told her to buy me an aeroplane. She burst out laughing and exclaimed, "You know that I can't even afford to buy you a bicycle". After that conversation, she departed, but later did something that surprised me.

She suddenly came back driving a brand new car. In my surprise, I asked to know how she had managed to buy herself a new car and she told me a challenging story. She had gone from house to house preaching the gospel. In one particular house, she preached to a rich man who gave his life to Christ and became so filled with the joy of salvation that he decided to do something for this sister. Since money was not a problem for him, he purchased a brand new car and offered it to the sister as a gift in appreciation of her ministry leading to the salvation of his soul.

What God did for that sister, He can do for you today. There is a fish in your neighbourhood waiting to be caught, and if only you go out and speak of Christ to your neighbours, you will experience the ultimate financial breakthrough. The man of God instructed the woman to gather empty vessels and she did. Do you know that God has already planned your breakthrough even before you cry unto him? Unknown to the widow, God had already provided all the empty vessels she would need. The only thing was that the vessels needed collecting from her neighbours. When she asked for the vessels, she obtained as many as she needed without any struggle.

The Bible says;

And it shall come to pass, that before they call, I will answer; and while they are yet speaking, I will hear. Isaiah 65:24

God said before you even call, He will answer. He knows the end from the beginning and has planned and provided everything you need to experience the ultimate financial breakthrough. If you believe this and act wisely, your journey to greatness can begin instantly.

Chapter Five

STEPS TO UNLIMITED GREATNESS

Unlimited greatness comes when certain steps are taken. The widow took two decisive steps: The first step she took was to release the only bottle of oil she had. She had one full bottle and decided to let it go. I am sure you know that when you pour oil from a bottle into a very big container and you attempt to pour the oil back into the bottle, you will never get a full bottle again. Some of the oil will be lost inside the big container.

The widow did not take the possibility of losing some of her oil into consideration. She believed totally in the God of

Elisha and she was blessed with a miracle. Though she did not have much oil, she believed the word of the man of God and acted accordingly. The Bible says;

Thus saith the LORD; Cursed be the man that trusteth in man, and maketh flesh his arm, and whose heart departeth from the LORD.

For he shall be like the heath in the desert, and shall not see when good cometh; but shall inhabit the parched places in the wilderness, in a salt land and not inhabited.

Blessed is the man that trusteth in the LORD, and whose hope the LORD is.

For he shall be as a tree planted by the waters, and that spreadeth out her roots by the river, and shall not see when heat cometh, but her leaf shall be green; and shall not be careful in the year of drought, neither shall cease from yielding fruit: Jeremiah 17:5-8

It pays to put absolute confidence in God. When the Almighty God tells you to sow and you don't act accordingly, then you will not be blessed. If you lack faith in God, you will be reluctant to sow any seed whatsoever, but unless you give God what you have, you cannot receive what you need from Him.

SACRIFICIAL GIVING

A poor widow attended one of our programmes and decided to give in spite of her poverty. After the death of her husband she had struggled to feed seventeen people who were directly under her care. A word of knowledge was uttered that someone would receive three breakthroughs. God stated that the first one belonged to Him, the second was to be divided equally and the third to be taken by the recipient. When the woman received the first breakthrough, she came to me and said: "I am the one whom God spoke about; Here is the money", I told her that God was not referring to her and tried to make her understand that she needed all the money she could get at the time.

But the woman surprised me when she said, "I'm sure you would not like me to miss my blessing. If I'm not faithful with this initial breakthrough, the second and the third will not come". I collected the money from her and encouraged her faith. After a short time, the second breakthrough came, as well as the third, just as she had believed.

God has promoted the poor widow and today she is a director in one of the biggest Banks in Nigeria.

HARD WORK

The widow released her oil because she trusted God, and she prospered as a result of this singular act. Pouring oil from one container to another requires hard work. She did not pour the oil into a few containers and then claim that she was tired, but she kept on pouring and working hard until she had filled every available container with oil. When God grants you a special breakthrough, you will need to work very hard. The Bible says that God is the rewarder of those who diligently seek him. You may be happy being lazy if you are not interested in securing the ultimate financial breakthrough. But if you want this breakthrough, you must be ready for hard work.

I went through some challenging experiences several years ago. I had been taught, as had others, that if you pay your tithes and offerings, then God would prosper you financially. As a scientist and mathematician, I pondered in my mind whether that teaching was plausible. I was a university lecturer, and I knew that my salary was fixed.

However, I obeyed God and He surprised me by opening many doors of blessing. Some secondary schools located around the University of Lagos where I lectured needed a competent teacher to deliver some special lectures on mathematics on a part-time basis. I applied and before I knew what was happening, I was given part-time jobs in three prominent secondary schools. Additionally, the university where I lectured developed some specialised academic subjects, and the participants insisted that I must be the one to teach them. At end of the day, the money I was taking home from the part-time jobs was more than a double of my monthly salary at the university. I had to work very hard, but the money kept coming into my pocket every month.

If you are praying for the ultimate financial breakthrough, you must get ready for hard work.

THE IMPORTANCE OF GRATITIUDE

The widow came back to the man of God with gratitude and she testified to the goodness of God in her life. If you want not just to experience but also to retain the ultimate financial breakthrough, you must manifest the spirit of gratitude. She was able to receive additional information from the man of God because she did the right things necessary to enjoy an enduring supernatural breakthrough.

The problem today is that when many people receive a small blessing, they forget the source of that blessing. A young man once came to me and asked for prayer that he might win a particular contract. I did. But, when I saw him a second time, I asked him, "Young man, you did not come back to tell me anything about the contract you asked me to pray about when you came forward for prayer". He mumbled and said; "Yes, I actually got the contract and I give glory to God". Then I told him, "You were zealously desperate when you needed divine intervention. How come you did not come back with the same zeal and give gratitude to God".

GIVE THANKS

If you want to keep your blessings, you must give thanks to God with a grateful heart. It is this attitude that will provoke God to bless you afresh. Believe the Lord and your quest for the ultimate financial breakthrough can be fulfilled.

Prayer Guide

1. Father, this month, guide me to my breakthrough in the name of Jesus.

2. Raise an offering and pray in this manner: Father, as I release this offering to you, let the door of my breakthrough begin to open in the name of Jesus.

Chapter Six

———◆———

THE KEY TO ABUNDANCE

And the word of the LORD came unto him, saying,

Arise, get thee to Zarephath, which beiongeth to Zidon, and dwell there: behold, I have commanded a widow woman there to sustain thee.

So he arose and went to Zarephath. And when he came to the gate of the city, behold, the widow woman was there gathering of sticks: and he called to her, and said, Fetch me, I pray thee, a little water in a vessel, that I may drink.

And as she was going to fetch it, he called to her, and said, Bring me, I pray thee, a morsel of bread in thine hand.

And she said, As the LORD thy God liveth, I have not a cake, but an handful of meal in a barrel, and a little oil in a cruse: and, behold, I am gathering two sticks, that I may go in and dress it for me and my son, that we may eat it, and die.

And Elijah said unto her, Fear not; go and do as thou hast said: but make me thereof a little cake first, and bring it unto me, and after make for thee and for thy son.

For thus saith the LORD God of Israel, The barrel of meal shall not waste, neither shall the cruse of oil fail, until the day that the LORD sendeth rain upon the earth.

And she went and did according to the saying of Elijah: and she, and he, and her house, did eat many days.

And the barrel of meal wasted not, neither did the cruse of oil fail, according to the word of the LORD, which he spake by Elijah. 1 Kings 17:8-16

I have good news for you in this chapter. From now on, you will never lack and your pocket will never be empty. From now until the end of your life, you will live in the realm of abundance. You will have the best food on your table and you will not lack good clothes to wear. God will give you cars to drive and will build houses for you. So prepare yourself for these divine surprises.

The passage of scripture above sets out the story of a woman who was once in a hopeless situation. However, her situation changed dramatically through an encounter with the Almighty. She was about to prepare her last meal and eat before death came. Miraculously, she survived, and the story of her survival teaches us that there is always hope for the hopeless. The Bible says;

To whom God would make known what is the riches of the glory of this mystery among the Gentiles; which is Christ in you, the hope of glory Colossians 1:27

As long as Christ remains in you there is a glorious future ahead of you. And even, before you finish reading this book, the glory of God will begin to shine in your life.

HELP FROM ABOVE

The widow woman had no inkling, whatsoever, about the direction from which help was to come. The Psalmist declares:

> *I will lift up mine eyes unto the hills,*
> *from whence cometh my help.*
> *My help cometh from the LORD, which*
> *made heaven and earth. Psalm 121:1-2*

God, the maker of Heaven and earth will send help to you today. The woman did not know that help was already on the way but God, the source of true help, had spoken to the prophet. He had to raise the prophet in order to allow a widow to enjoy the benefits of a divine encounter. God can raise anybody in order to bless you. In His wisdom and power, he can turn circumstances around and prepare the ground for a supernatural breakthrough.

The mystery behind the workings of God cannot be understood. God knew all that He was going to do in the life of the widow but He gave to Elijah only limited information about her. For instance, God did not give the name of the widow to Elijah. There were lots of widows in the city but

God did not give any further information concerning the beneficiary of the miracle. God simply ordered him to go.

The prophet arrived at the nick of time to see the woman gathering sticks. God is always on time! The help you require from Him will always arrive at the nick of time because He is never late.

Chapter Seven

SACRIFICIAL GIVING

And it came to pass the day after, that he went into a city called Nain; and many of his disciples went with him, and much people.

Now when he came nigh to the gate of the city, behold, there was a dead man carried out, the only son of his mother, and she was a widow: and much people of the city was with her.

And when the Lord saw her, he had compassion on her, and said unto her, Weep not.

And he came and touched the bier: and they that bare him stood still. And he said, Young man, I say unto thee, Arise.

And he that was dead sat up, and began to speak. And he delivered him to his mother. Luke 7:11-15

A widow was on her way to bury her dead son, but before she reached the graveyard, Jesus arrived just in time. God will reach you sooner than your expectation. The help you are expecting from Him will arrive at the exact time He has planned. The widow must have decided to accept the sad situation, and had planned her son's burial, but God stepped in.

THE DEADLINE

Let me share an interesting story with you. A sister and her blind mother were living in a rented apartment, but because they were badly in arrears with their rent, the landlord arrived one day and angrily gave them an ultimatum. He declared: "If by 12 noon tomorrow you have not paid your rent, I will throw you and your belongings out of my house". The lady prayed thus, with tears in her eyes: "O Lord, where will I go with my blind mother? O God, you have up to12 noon tomorrow to send help to us". She prayed out her heart until night time, when she fell asleep. When she woke up in the morning, she perceived the aroma of freshly made breakfast coming from the kitchen. She wondered if someone had climbed into their kitchen and was making breakfast. She got up to see who it was that had made breakfast.

THE AMAZING MIRACLE

To her surprise, it was her blind mother! God had miraculously healed her blind mother during the night. She discovered that her mother's eyes were very clear. Basking in that joy, they sat down in the living room to have their breakfast. Something touched the sister at that point, and her faith grew so strong that she prayed again, saying: "O God, if you can open my mother's eyes, then I know that the money with which we shall pay the rent will arrive before 12 noon". As God would have it, a postman pressed the doorbell as they were about to finish their breakfast and brought in with a letter containing a cheque. When they looked at the cheque, they discovered that it was not only sufficient to pay the rent but enough to buy the house as well.

Perhaps you are reading this book and you are struggling

with huge debts; I tell you that within a very short time, every debt which frightens you will be paid by God in the name of Jesus.

THE DIVINE CHOICE

God selected one particular widow, whose account we are studying, for a miracle. There were many widows in Zarephath, but this particular widow was singled out for the ultimate financial breakthrough. The Bible says;

> But I tell you of a truth, many widows were in Israel in the days of Elias, when the heaven was shut up three years and six months, when great famine was throughout all the land;

> But unto none of them was Elias sent, save unto Sarepta, a city of Sidon, unto a woman that was a widow. Luke 4:25-26

Why was this widow of Zarephath chosen by God for the ultimate financial breakthrough? What does God look for when He wants to grant you the ultimate financial breakthrough? What quality did God find in that widow that made her to be singled out as the privileged beneficiary of a life-changing divine encounter? The simple answer is this: the act of giving.

BENEFITS OF GIVING

God knew the woman was a giver. I believe that God must have told Elijah to look out for this when he got to Zarephath. He must have told Elijah to look out for a woman with a generous heart as a sign by which he would know that it was the right woman. I imagine God telling Elijah:

"When you ask such a woman for water in that town where there had been no rainfall for a very long time, she will willingly give you some even at such a time of chronic scarcity. When you see any woman who demonstrates this uncommon virtue, she is the one I have sent you to". Whenever God asks you to give Him something, you should see it as an indication that you are being tested.

THE REWARD

If you pass the test, certain benefits will be your reward that are far bigger than you can imagine. This widow was not just a giver but was a sacrificial giver. Initially the man of God asked for just a cup of water after which he made an additional request for a meal. The woman told Elijah that there was just one meal left to feed her entire household. It was a very big test when the man of God said, "Offer me that meal". The woman did not grumble, but she gave it sacrificially.

THE WIDOW'S MITE?

Some believers have formed the habit of saying; "This is my widow's mite!" I was once guilty of using this misleading phrase until God corrected me. God told me never to refer to any gift as a widow's mite unless I have given all that I have. The mite that was given by the widow was her entire possession. If you want to give a small amount of your financial resources, you had better say: "This is a miser's gift". To say that you are giving a widow's mite is to say that you are giving the totality of your resources.

The widow of Zarephath gave her last meal simply because her trust in God was so great.

The man of God said, "Give me my meal first and then the Lord will surprise you". Elijah proclaimed God's blessing on her when he said that she would never lack food in her household. The woman must have believed that the God who could bring water out of the rock and send manna from Heaven could also work in her situation. She knew that God can do the impossible. Like the widow, you must learn to trust God today and He, the great provider, will meet all your needs in the name of Jesus.

God taught me very deep lessons in the areas of giving several years ago, when there was a great need in the church. We were trying to roof the extension of the auditorium located at the entrance of the redemption camp, which would cost 17,000 (about one hundred dollars). One of our regional pastors also needed 1,000 (about seven dollars) to roof one of the church buildings. Interestingly, I had 1,000 and I was wondering where I would get 16,000 to make up the money needed for the roofing.

The pastor came and pleaded passionately with me and saying, "I need 1,000 to roof the dormitory". I wondered why he had come to ask me for 1,000, because my own need was very urgent. I told him to stop disturbing me as I was in need of 16,000. The pastor got up and left my office. Meanwhile, I became restless. It was then that God spoke to me and said, "Give him 1,000". This was not an easy thing for me to do, but because God had spoken, I had to obey. I called the pastor and gave him 1,000.

All the money I had was gone. I watched the pastor depart full of joy, but I was very sad. God spoke to me then and said, "My son what is your problem? There were two needs to be met. I have dealt with one, and that leaves just one more. Leave the problem to me and I will surprise you". True to God's word, somebody came all the way from Port Harcourt to my office and said that he had just received some rent from his house. He said that God had commanded him in unmistakable terms to come and give the money to me. He handed a fat envelope to me and I sat down with joy while I opened it. I counted the money and it was exactly 17,000. When I gave the only one thousand Naira I had to the area pastor, I had no idea where the 17,000 would come from that I needed to roof the auditorium. God, in His greatness, raised up help from far away Port Harcourt. Give to God, and He will send help to you from places you never imagined. Give whenever God prompts you to do so, and watch Him surprise you.

PRAYER GUIDE

1. My father, show me the way to the ultimate financial breakthrough.

2. Oh God, show me the secret of exceptional prosperity.

3. Father, let your well of prosperity flow into my life in Jesus name.

4. My father, connect me to the source of my breakthrough in Jesus name.

Chapter Eight

---◆◆◆---

THE PATHWAY TO RICHES

So he departed thence, and found Elisha the son of Shaphat, who was plowing with twelve yoke of oxen before him, and he with the twelfth: and Elijah passed by him, and cast his mantle upon him.

And he left the oxen, and ran after Elijah, and said, Let me, I pray thee, kiss my father and my mother, and then I will follow thee. And he said unto him, Go back again: for what have I done to thee?

And he returned back from him, and took a yoke of oxen,

and slew them, and boiled their flesh with the instruments of the oxen, and gave unto the people, and they did eat. Then he arose, and went after Elijah, and ministered unto him. 1 Kings 19:19-21

Elisha was rich by present day standards. He was the son of the wealthiest farmer who lived at the time. If we are to use the language of modern agriculture, Elijah's father had twelve tractors on his large farm. A farmer who has twelve tractors must, without doubt, be classified as a multi-millionaire.

THE BEST IS YET TO COME

Though Elisha was rich, he did not know that God had something greater for him. For much of the time, people often hold on to what is good and miss out on what is better for them. Those who have experienced a degree of financial prosperity settle for the minimum, while the maximum is there for the asking.

It is tragic when those who achieve a reasonable level of prosperity conclude that there is no greater level to attain. Some people climb a few rungs on the ladder of progress and settle down when there are other greater heights they could attain.

GREATER ASPIRATIONS

If Elisha had decided to live the rest of his life relying on his father's wealth and achievements, he would have died and been forgotten. Elisha received some form of spiritual enlightenment. He knew that his father's great wealth could only be regarded as a springboard for his future prosperity. I have discovered that those who work hardest are often those who have little or nothing to fall back upon. The children of the super-rich are always busy doing nothing. They do not consider the fact that they can improve on the riches which they inherited from their father.

If Elisha had settled for the level of wealth he inherited from his father, he would not have come anywhere near becoming a notable character in the Bible. To achieve the ultimate financial breakthrough, you need to consider your present level as the minimum. With this mindset, you will be well prepared for uncommon greatness.

The Bible says;

> But as it is written, Eye hath not seen, nor ear heard, neither have entered into the heart of man, the things which God hath prepared for them that love him.

But God hath revealed them unto us by his Spirit: for the Spirit searcheth all things, yea, the deep things of God. 1 Corinthians 2:9-10

God is going to take you to a level of prosperity that can only be described as unimaginable. When a person's acquisition of wealth is seen as unprecedented, it fits into the mould of the above passage.

A GLORIOUS PLAN

The Almighty has planned to bless you with the greatest level of wealth attainable. Elisha thought he was wealthy, but he did not know that a day was coming when kings would serve him and call him "Father!" He thought he was going to die a rich farmer but God had a different plan for him. In the same vein, God has a glorious plan for you. Before you leave this world, presidents will serve you!

Elisha was wise. He traded his current level of wealth for a greater one by allowing God to have His way in his life. Elisha decided to surrender sugar for honey. On the day the mantle of Elijah fell upon him, his destiny changed. God brought him into the realm of the ultimate financial breakthrough. He knew then that to receive ultimate breakthrough from God, he needed to surrender what he was holding on to. You must offer God what appears to be your best at the present moment, so that He can give you what is better than your best.

God has precious honey in store for you. What you must do is surrender the little you are holding in your hands. If God were to show you the graphic details of the realm which He is talking to you about, you would be afraid.

You might wonder at how He will do it. How it will happen is God's business, not yours. God will make the impossible to become possible because He is the Almighty, the creator of heaven and earth. When you cannot see any way out, God will show you more than a million ways. He can give you a breakthrough even by using birds or animals. He can channel your breakthrough to you by using the resources of a king, a governor or a president.

BLESSINGS FOR THE FAITHFUL

Each time I remember the story of the widow mentioned earlier on in chapter 5, I get surprised at the wonders of God. This widow had difficulties and had to live on her meagre resources. She attended a meeting where a prophetic utterance was made. God gave her three specific instructions. Prior to her encounter with the Almighty, she was heavily in debt, but in spite of this she had to feed seventeen people.

God stated that somebody would receive three miracles of financial prosperity. The first miracle must be handed over to Him completely, the second was to be shared equally, with God taking a half. The third miracle would be kept for the beneficiary of the miracle and with that third miracle the beneficiary would forget forever her life of poverty.

The woman claimed the prophecy, and when the first miracle came, she came with all the proceeds and said, "I'm offering all this to God in obedience to his word". I told her that she had probably made a mistake because God could be referring to her because of her pitiful financial predicament. I even tried to convince her that God did not mention her name when that word of knowledge was uttered. She said, "Do you want to deprive me of the other two miracles? You must accept this offering if you want to see me out of my financial doldrums".

When I realised that she was so persistent, I accepted the money but because I was so moved by her predicament, I did not use her money for any of the Church projects. I kept it just in case she decided to come for it.

The second breakthrough came and the woman divided the proceeds into two equal halves. She took
one half and gave the other half to God. And because she remained faithful, the third miracle came and she attained the ultimate level of breakthrough.

AMAZING!

When the husband of the widow died, he had left behind a huge debt. There was a bank in the United Kingdom which, according to its records, claimed he owed it a large sum of money. One day, the bank wrote a letter to the widow which stated: "We have made a serious mistake. After scrutinizing the books, we discovered that your husband does not owe the bank a penny. Rather, it is the bank which owes your husband a huge amount of money". Wonderful! How can a bank in the United Kingdom make a mistake? If you ask me, I would rather say that God decided to change the books in order to bless the woman financially. That was how the bank in the United Kingdom paid the widow a huge amount of money which made her stupendously rich.

How will God give you your own miracle? What will God do to make you rich? I don't really know. However, what I do know is that God can do anything just to bless you. Whatever He has promised, He will definitely fulfil to the letter.

Chapter Nine

THE TURNAROUND MIRACLE

Elisha was blessed with a turnaround miracle. He made a step of faith, involving great sacrifice and God blessed him beyond his wildest dreams. One of the qualities which earned him his great breakthrough is that he was hard working. Even if God decides to bless you today, there is a level you may never get to if you are lazy. Those who want extraordinary blessings must be prepared to work hard extraordinarily. The Bible says;

Seest thou a man diligent in his business? he shall stand before kings;

he shall not stand before mean men. Proverbs 22:29

Elisha was busy working hard. He did not lie down lazily and command his father's labourers to work their fingers to the bone for him. He kept working alongside his father's labourers.

So he departed thence, and found Elisha the son of Shaphat, who was plowing with twelve yoke of oxen before him, and he with the twelfth: and Elijah passed by him, and cast his mantle upon him. 1 Kings 19:19

THE DIGNITY OF LABOUR

Anyone who desires a divine breakthrough must be ready to work hard. All the disciples of Jesus were hard working. He called each one of them while they were in the pathway of duty. Peter was an experienced and skilful fisherman before the Lord called him. Matthew was working in his tax collector's booth when the Lord called him.

Becoming a Christian does not exempt anyone from hard work. None of the disciples of Jesus were idle at the time they were called. I had a good number of friends when I became a believer. Some of them were so lazy that although they talked big, they were not prepared for hard work. We were all taught the principles of faith and positive confession but I knew that achieving greatness in life goes beyond mere confessions.

EMPTY CONFESSIONS

My friends cultivated the habit of saying: "I am the head and not the tail: I shall prosper and lend to nations, I will never borrow" etc. They made such confessions without any corresponding labour to back them up: Some of them spent five years making confessions like, "I am a millionaire and I possess a good car by faith". At the end of the day, they remained as poor as they were at the beginning of their confessions.

If you refuse to work and you go about confessing that you have claimed the car of your dreams by faith, the only car you will end up with will be your two legs.

THE SOWER'S SEED

Elisha was generous; he was not remotely miserly. As soon as he was called, he prepared a feast and fed his people. The Bible says;

There is that scattereth, and yet increaseth; and there is that withholdeth more than is meet, but it tendeth to poverty.

The liberal soul shall be made fat: and he that watereth shall be watered also himself. Proverbs 11:24-25

Elisha was so generous that he decided to show benevolence to his people. God knew that he was a giver. That was why He gave him such abundant blessings. God does not release His wealth into the hands of misers. He delights in bestowing his blessings upon people who are channels of blessings. The elders have a saying that the secrets of the giver will never come to the open, but those of the miser are never covered. In other words, if you are generous, God will keep on supplying your needs. The Bible says it another way, thus:

For as the rain cometh down, and the snow from heaven, and returneth not thither, but watereth the earth, and maketh it bring forth and bud, that it may give seed to the sower, and bread to the eater: Isaiah 55:10
Now he that ministereth seed to the sower both minister bread for your food, and multiply your seed sown, and increase the fruits of your righteousness; 2 Corinthians 9:10

God will always give the willing sower enough seed to sow. The moment you have the spirit of giving you will never lack enough seed to sow. Some people who need a breakthrough may be poor today but I know that God will bless them because such people have a great desire to become channels of blessings to others.

CONDITIONS FOR MORE BLESSINGS

A believer may hitchhike or commute by bus in order to attend a Christian meeting, but if such a believer would say, "Oh God, if only you will provide a big bus for me, I will make it available or those who have no means to transport themselves but are willing to attend this meeting", I tell you, God will quickly endow such a person with the wherewithal to buy a bus. Some people are blessed with vehicles but they ignore those who are trying to hitch a ride to Christian meetings. If such misers keep asking God to bless them with an aircraft, I believe God will simply ignore them.

If you ask God for something bigger, He will ask what you have done with the previous blessings which He gave to you. God watches meticulously and measures the motives behind your actions.

If you fail to make use of simple opportunities, God may never give you bigger ones. But my prayer is that God will bestow on you the grace to be generous.

PRAYER GUIDE

1. My father lead me into uncommon greatness.

2. Father, take me to the realm of ultimate financial breakthrough.

3. My father and my God, bless me with abundant financial provision.

4. O Lord, make me your financial treasurer.

Chapter Ten

—▸◆◂—

UNCOMMON PROSPERITY

One of the qualities which qualified Elisha for an exceptional financial breakthrough was his devotion to serving the servant of God, Elijah. The Bible states that Elisha poured water on Elijah's hand. From this it is clear that there are lots of blessings reserved for those who serve God's prophet. The Bible says;

He that receiveth a prophet in the name of a prophet shall receive a prophet's reward; and he that receiveth a righteous man in the name of a righteous man shall receive a righteous man's reward.

And whosoever shall give to drink unto one of these little ones a cup of cold water only in the name of a disciple, verily I say unto you, he shall in no wise lose his reward. Matthew 10:41-42

You can serve a man of God without getting anything in return. When a man of God pronounces blessing on you by saying "God bless you", he is not just paying you a compliment. A casual "God bless you" from a friend is not the same as "God bless you" from a man of God. A "God bless you" from a man of God is loaded with prophetic blessings. Hence you must be ready to do the things which will qualify you for a divine benediction. When you serve a man of God, a simple "God bless you" will load you with tremendous blessings.

A TESTIMONY

Recently, I was in the United States of America and one of my sons in the Lord shared his testimony. He testified thus: "God surprised me during the General Overseer's previous visit. Prior to the his arrival, the pastor called me and told me that he had chosen me as the one who would drive him during his visit. I tried to explain to the pastor that it might not be easy for me to take up the assignment since I was preparing for a major examination. But the pastor insisted that I would drive the General Overseer all the same.

"I thought I could manage to combine driving the General Overseer around with preparing to write the crucial examination because I thought that the he would spend just one day here. To my surprise, the he stayed a whole week."

"When he was finally leaving, he simply said "God bless you". And to the glory of God, I passed my exams in flying colours and I got a new job and prospered tremendously."

"Now that the G.O General Overseer is here on another ministerial visit, I must be the one to drive him".

BLESSINGS GALORE

Another brother also experienced uncommon breakthrough after driving me around when I visited Dallas Texas, in America. When I was leaving after the programme I gave some money to those who had cooked and served my meals. I turned to the brother who drove me and said, "As for you, you don't need money. God bless you". Later when he shared his testimony he said, "The only problem I have today is how to spend the money God has blessed me with. God has given me so much money that I really don't know how to spend it".

Elisha was committed to the business of the kingdom. And so when the man of God, Elijah, asked to know what Elisha wanted, he had only one answer: A double portion of the power of God that rested on Elijah. The Bible says;

But seek ye first the kingdom of God, and his righteousness; and ail these things shall be added unto you. Matthew 6:33

God is looking for those who are concerned about the business of the kingdom. He is looking for those who are desperate to extend the frontiers of God's kingdom on earth. God is searching for men and women who are addicted to the expansion of His kingdom.

COMMITMENT TO THE KINGDOM'S BUSINESS

If you are concerned with the progress of the kingdom of God, God will single you out and bless you. If your major preoccupation is the evangelization of the lost and the growth of the church, then God will bless you with the ultimate financial breakthrough. God is seeking divine treasurers. He is looking for men and women who are ready to expend their resources on the propagation of the gospel. God will make such people multi-millionaires.

You are not ready for uncommon financial blessings until you have settled the issue of your involvement in the kingdom's business. When God discovers that you are praying for resources which you want to invest in His work, He will be very quick to bless you. God will only give a major breakthrough to those whose primary concern is His work.

I learnt the importance of making God's work my first priority when I was very young in the Lord. In December 1973, I was faced with the challenge of having to demonstrate my preference for the work of the Lord. I had just finished writing my Ph.D. thesis and was meant to stay behind and defend it in an oral examination. Those who are in academic circles know the importance of the viva. But when I was preparing for it, a challenge came up in the church.

My father-in-the-Lord, the late Pa. Akindayomi, the founder of the Redeemed Christian Church of God, informed me that a crusade had been scheduled to take place at Ilesha, a town in the Western Nigeria and that my presence there was very important. My father in the Lord told me specifically that he wished to be housed in my personal apartment in Ilesha during the programme. I quickly responded that I would go with him along with the other top ministers.

Meanwhile, I knew that it was the time I was expected to settle down seriously and prepare for the oral examinations. However, as far as I was concerned, the work of God was my utmost priority. While I was in Ilesha participating in the crusade, my Head of Department was busy marking my PhD thesis.

DIVINE INTERVENTION

As soon as the H.O.D was through with the grading, he took my project to the external examiner. The external examiner was so impressed that he told my H.O.D. that he should go ahead and award me a PhD degree. The other lecturers quickly raised objections saying that I had not participated in the viva. He simply stated that as far as my thesis was concerned, there was no need for an oral examination. The other lecturers stated that such an exemption had never been granted anyone in the history of the university. The external examiner simply stated that as long as he was the one in authority he was determined that I should be awarded a Ph.D degree, oral or no oral examination. He said that he had no questions for me and that I was eligible for a Ph.D degree, judging by my brilliant performance.

If I were a woman, the people would have accused the lecturer of having being seduced by his female student. If the lecturer were to have been a Christian, others would have accused him of being partial. But the man was a vehement unbeliever. I never knew him from my previous life. In fact I never came across him again until twenty years after. God simply used a heathen to bless me. And so when you do God's work, he will take care of your concerns. When you serve Him, He will bless you financially.

FAITHFULNESS

Finally, Elisha experienced uncommon breakthrough because he was faithful to the end. He served Elijah till the end. He didn't serve him for a short while and then abandon him; rather he kept serving until Elijah was taken away.

To receive extraordinary breakthrough, therefore you must be faithful to God till the end. Remember, God knows the end from the beginning. He knows those who will be faithful till the end. God will give such people a type of prosperity that will never end. If you want God to prosper you tremendously, you must exhibit the qualities described in this Chapter

Other Books by the Author

THE LAST DAYS
GOD THE HOLY SPIRIT
DAVID VOLUME 1
DAVID VOLUME 2
ARRESTING THE ARRESTER
SPIRITUAL GIFTS
WHEN YOU NEED A MIRACLE
JOSEPH
AVENGE ME OF MY ADVERSARIES
THE HOLY SPIRIT
IN THE LIFE OF PETER
THE SIEGE IS OVER
I KNOW WHO I AM
TURNING POINT
SHOWER OF BLESSINGS
SERMON OF THE HOLY GHOST SERVICE
THE ALMIGHTY
HOLY SPIRIT
IN THE LIFE OF ELIJAH
THE LORD IS MY SHEPHERD
THE LAST DAY OF ELIJAH
THE TEN VIRGIN
THE HIDING PLACE

TOTAL SANCTIFICATION
65 KEYS TO PROSPERITY
YOUR TOMORROW WILL BE ALRIGHT
HELP FROM ABOVE
THE WATER AND THE FIRE
IN HIS PRESENCE
DIVINE RELATIONSHIP
OUR DOMINION CROWN
JESUS THE LORD OF UNIVERSE
THE TALE OF THREE WOMEN
BEHOLD HE COMETH
JOURNEY TO MARRIAGE
PRAY WITHOUT CEASING
GOD CAN CHANGE YOUR SONG
CHILD OF DESTINY
DIVINE ENCOUNTER
THE CRUCIFIED LIFE
GOD HAS PURPOSE FOR YOUR LIFE
THE BRIDE OF THE LAMB
FOLLOW-UP IN EVANGELISM
A HANDBOOK ON PERSONAL EVANGELISM
THE AWESOME GOD
UNCOMMON GREATNESS
THE MASTER KEY
AND LOT MORE

Notes

Notes